The BEDTIME Leunig

The BEDTIME Leunig

..... Michael Leunig

ANGUS & ROBERTSON PUBLISHERS

ANGUS & ROBERTSON PUBLISHERS
London • Sydney • Melbourne • Singapore • Manila

This book is copyright. Apart from any fair dealing for the
purposes of private study, research, criticism or review, as
permitted under the Copyright Act, no part may be reproduced
by any process without written permission. Inquiries should
be addressed to the publishers.

First published by Angus & Robertson Publishers, Australia, 1981

© Michael Leunig 1981

National Library of Australia
Cataloguing-in-publication data.

Leunig, Michael.
 The bedtime Leunig.
 ISBN 0 207 14505 9.

 1. Australian wit and humor, Pictorial.
 2. Caricatures and cartoons — Australia. I. Title.
741.5'994

Printed in Hong Kong

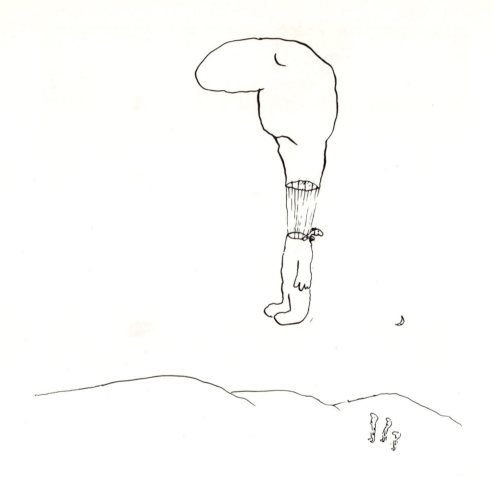

SOMETIMES AT NIGHT I THINK ABOUT
THE HUMAN FACE... THE
MOST MYSTERIOUS SURFACE
ON EARTH

ALL THE FACES I KNOW
MERGE TOGETHER INTO
ONE FACE ... THE
AMALGAMATED FACE
SEEN ABOVE IN PROFILE.

I LIE THERE FACE TO FACE
WITH THE AMALGAMATED FACE.
WE STARE BLANKLY AT
EACH OTHER.

I SEARCH THE AMALGAMATED
FACE FOR SOME EXPRESSION... .
A FAINT SMILE... A WINK....
A FROWN .... A TEAR ...

BUT THE AMALGAMATED FACE
GIVES NOTHING AWAY. IT IS
COMPOSED AND BLANK.
WHAT CAN IT MEAN...?

LIFE ON EARTH

OWLS HAVE NO NEW YEAR'S EVE....

NEITHER CAN THEIR LIVES BE MEASURED IN DAYS...

FOR THEY ARE FOWLS OF THE NIGHT

 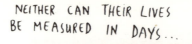

THEY ARE NEVER MENTIONED IN NEW YEAR HONORS LISTS. OWLS ARE BORN WITH HONOR...!

THEY MAKE NO NEW YEAR RESOLUTIONS... INSTINCTIVE CREATURES DON'T NEED RESOLUTION.

THEY TAKE NO HOSTAGES, NO DRUGS NO HOLIDAYS, NO SHOWERS.

IF IT FEELS GOOD... DO IT

NO WORRIES

OWLS IGNORE

ART
RELIGION
POLITICS
SPORT
CLOTHES
MEDIA
WATER SKIING

MUSIC
AGRICULTURE
HISTORY
GOLD
FURNITURE
WORLD TRAVEL
UNIONISM
PHOTO ALBUMS

IDENTIKIT PORTRAITS
MAPS
TELEPHONES
CHARITY
SCANDAL
FASHION
OMENS

OWLS LIKE

TREES
MOONLIGHT
SEX
FOOD
NESTS
HOOTING

VOTE
[1]

OWLS

Leunig

THE EVOLUTION THEORY

SOME LIFE FORMS EVOLVED
INTO HUMANS....

... AND OTHERS DEVELOPED INTO
ARM CHAIRS

WHILE OTHERS AGAIN BECAME
COLOR TELEVISION SETS.

WHICH ALL CAME TOGETHER AS
THE WONDROUS BALANCE OF NATURE
WE KNOW TODAY

There was a comedian whose sense of humor became so damaged that he could not earn a living.

He claimed workers compensation and tried to prove to a court how a series of emotional accidents had rendered him unfunny.

His evidence described a lifetime of exhilarating joys and sudden jolting heartbreaks which caused "philosophical whiplash"

This condition caused the business of being funny to be very difficult... and it was hard to take things seriously too... the confusion was crippling.

MAN TRIPPING

BANANA SKIN   CONFUSION

The court howled with laughter...

The case was dismissed...

COURT

ARISE....
LORD
MUCK...

CUDDLY
POSSUMS

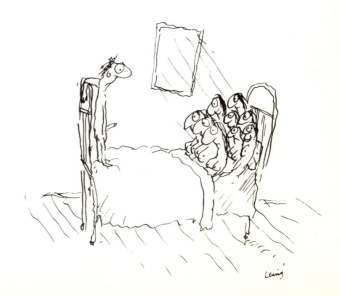

MODERN QUEEN SCOUTS

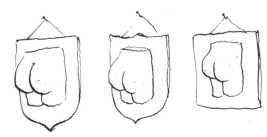

CAN I INTEREST YOU IN THIS GLASS OF NOTHING...?

NO THANKS.. I'VE ALREADY HAD PLENTY OF NOTHING..

THE RECYCLING REVOLUTION

MACRAMÉ THIS UNIQUE SMOKING JACKET FROM THOSE UNWANTED POTATO PEELINGS AND AMAZE YOUR FRIENDS

FERAL HUMAN HUNTING FOR PREY.

STANDBY CHECK IN

LAID BACK CHECK IN

PUT UP MY
HANDS FOR ME
THANKYOU JEEVES..

LOOSEN YOUR
BELTS FOR
TAKE OFF

MAFIA
GAME
40 CENTS
RESTRAINS
HAMMER

NOW YOU JUST WATCH
THE CHICKENS AND WE'LL
LEARN ABOUT THE
FACTS OF LIFE.

WATCH CLOSELY NOW..
HERE COMES THE ROOSTER..
JUST YOU WATCH HIM AND
ASK ME ANY QUESTIONS...

ERRR..
···WHY IS
THE ROOSTER
WEARING A
MASK AND
CARRYING
A KNIFE..?

Leunig

"SIRE . . . THE VASSALS ARE HASSLING THE CASTLE!"

  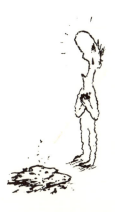

HEY THERE...
SLOW DOWN
DRIVER...

I AM THE ANGEL OF
HUMAN GRACE AND
INTEGRITY...

I NOTICE YOU ARE THE ONLY
PERSON IN THIS TRAFFIC JAM...
...IN THIS ENTIRE CITY...

...WHO IS NOT DISPLAYING
SOME FORM OF STUPID
DEMEANING BUMPER STICKER...
I SALUTE YOUR DIGNITY.

YOU HAVE JUST WON
A HASSLE FREE FLIGHT HOME
EVERY NIGHT FOR ONE WEEK..!

TO BEAUTIFY A FACTORY, A CLEVER ARCHITECT HAD THE BUILDING CLAD WITH MIRRORS

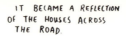

IT BECAME A REFLECTION OF THE HOUSES ACROSS THE ROAD.

THE HOUSE DWELLERS THOUGHT THE EFFECT WAS SO CLEVER THAT THEY TOO ERECTED MIRROR FACADES

THE TWO SETS OF MIRRORS REFLECTED EACH OTHER, BACK AND FORWARD ACROSS THE ROAD AT THE SPEED OF LIGHT.

A REFLECTION OF A REFLECTION OF INFINITE NOTHINGNESS. A VISUAL VACUUM.

THIS BEAUTIFICATION.. THIS ELIMINATION OF REALITY WAS SUCH A RELIEF THAT THE ENTIRE CITY WAS CLAD AND PAVED WITH MIRRORS.

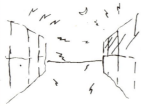

IT SEEMS RIDICULOUS BUT EVEN THE CITIZENS TOOK TO WEARING SPECIAL MIRROR CLOTHING

ALL THAT SEEMED TO REMAIN WAS THE SOUNDS OF THE CITY... AND A VAST SKY WHICH WAS HALF COVERED WITH MARKS WHERE THE MIRRORS JOINED

LIFE HAD BECOME A DEAFENING REFLECTION OF NOTHING IN PARTICULAR.

leunig

AN AUTUMN STORY...

An Adelaide "arty" type spoiling clean, Melbourne fun with his sneering smartness.

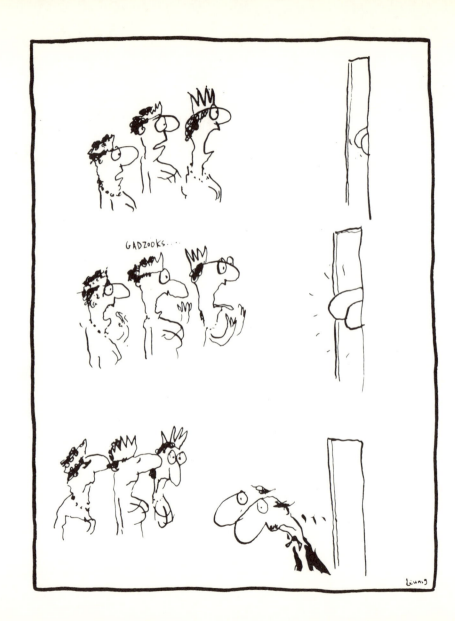

A lingering
bouquet.

HOME
UNCERTAIN
HOME

REX

PRINCE

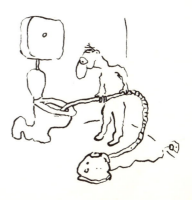

IT'S AN IDEAL BALANCE REALLY... BETWEEN THE BLACK HOLE OF CALCUTTA AND THE SEIGE OF STALINGRAD

STOP
STOP

THERE'S BEEN
A BIG MISTAKE...
.. ITS THE
WRONG
ONE... YOU'VE GOT
THE WRONG
ONE...

THAT'S THE SHARP
AXE ..... YOU SHOULD
BE USING THE
BLUNT ONE
ON THAT
BUGGER..

Leunig

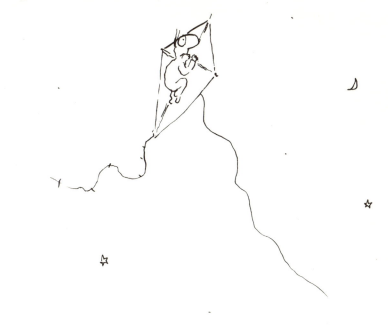

THANKYOU
FOR NOT
ENQUIRING

TURN BACK
YOU ARE
GOING THE
WRONG WAY.
IT'S ALL
BEEN DONE
BEFORE

YOUR MALIGNANT
DORSAL GROWTHS HAVE
BEEN DIAGNOSED AS
A SEVERE CASE OF _WINGS_

WHICH REQUIRE
JUST A SIMPLE
AMPUTATION

AND A
DRESSING OVER
THE WOUND
TO PREVENT
REGROWTH

LONDON, Wed. — An American stuntman hoping to become the first person to swim the English Channel with his hands and feet bound, gave up after only 6.4 km today.

I WAS INSPIRED

I decided to be the first human to climb Mount Everest bound and gagged...

I made it to the front gate of my Footscray home with NO PROBLEMS

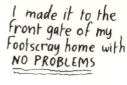

Then I fell down and rolled into the gutter...

it started to rain but I was undaunted... I had Mount Everest on the brain...

the gutter was awash and litter piled up around me..

THEN IT HAPPENED... The surging torrent pushed me forward.. I WAS ON MY WAY...!

After several hours I arrived at a drain about ten yards down the street. My head entered... I decided to establish a base camp..

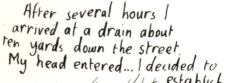

I fell asleep and dreamed wild joyous dreams about Everest which now lay within my grasp.

"GREAT DEEDS AND GREAT THOUGHTS ALL HAVE A RIDICULOUS BEGINNING."
— CAMUS

actually... my OWN PERSONAL ship never came in either...

... and it can't be salvaged because the wreckage is strewn too far and wide....

.... pieces fell off on the track to Mildura... ...bits were lost in New Guinea ....

The Orama Ballroom... The Royal Hotel... Footscray Park... all littered with fragments...

It broke up so gradually I never noticed...

... and I ended up in a barbed wire canoe..... life boat of the working class.

Leunig

why do you
tremble...

Because I'm
a precarious
person I think..

Life is so
shakey... the balance
is frightening

My thoughts quiver...
nothing is
firm.

I can't
from to

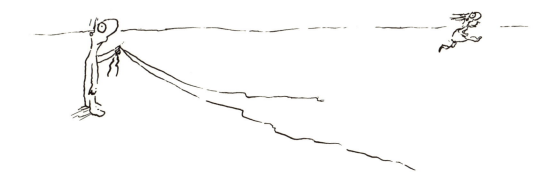

DOMESTIC ECLIPSES.

① Eclipse of the affections

Where person A moves
between persons B and C

② Total alcoholic eclipse

Complete blacking out
of consciousness...

③ Eclipse of innocence

The losing sight of
one's childhood....

④ Partial eclipse of the joke

Where sex, religion or politics
obscure the fact that it is
all a huge joke.....

⑤ Eclipse of the inevitable

A pleasant day can mask
from us the fact that one
day we will probably die
in a car accident...

⑥ Total eclipse of the feet

Leuniy

FROM THE AMAZING WATER POWERED CAR OF QUEENSLAND...

IT IS JUST A SHORT TECHNOLOGICAL STEP TO THE BREAD AND WATER POWERED CAR.

WHICH IS THE FORERUNNER OF THE COMPLETE GOURMET CAR POWERED BY THREE COURSE MEALS AND FRENCH WINES

Pierres

BY THIS TIME HUMANS, WHO ALREADY DRINK HERBICIDES DISCOVER THE JOYS OF DRINKING PETROL

HOWEVER... A STRANGE THING HAPPENS. TWO HUNDRED CHILDREN COLLAPSE MYSTERIOUSLY AT AN ENGLISH JAZZ FESTIVAL....

..AND BY A FANTASTIC COINCIDENCE IN ETHIOPIA, TWO THOUSAND CHILDREN COLLAPSE AT A HUNGER FESTIVAL AND ACTUALLY DIE...!

NEXT WEEK
THE QUEEN MOTHER RIDES AGAIN
WILD SCENES

12 APR 1980

THERE WAS ONCE A MAN
WHO HAD NEVER SEEN HIMSELF
BECAUSE HE HAD NO MIRROR

HE WOULD STARE AT THE WALL
WHERE THE MIRROR SHOULD HAVE
BEEN AND WONDER ABOUT WHO
HE WAS.

HE WOULD DREAM AND
DREAM ABOUT ALL THE
POSSIBILITIES

ONE DAY HE WAS GIVEN
A MIRROR AND HIS
DREAMS ENDED. HE
SAW TWO THINGS.

HE SAW HIMSELF.....

...AND HE SAW
NO POSSIBILITIES.

Leunig

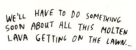

YOU CAN ALWAYS PICK THEM
BY THE LOOK IN THEIR EYE...

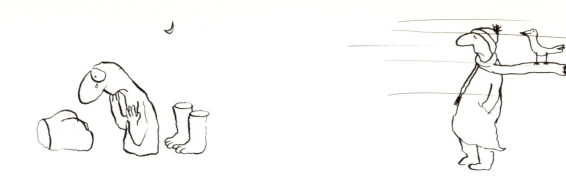

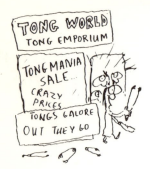

TONG WORLD
TONG EMPORIUM

TONG MANIA
SALE
CRAZY
PRICES
TONGS GALORE
OUT THEY GO

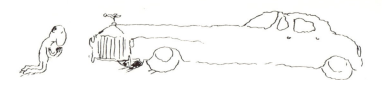

A WOMAN DROPS OUT
OF A TREE AND LANDS
ON ISAAC NEWTON... THUS
HE DISCOVERS THE LAW
OF DEPRAVITY.

AIR COOLED
BARBECUE FORK

seven minutes to midnight....
staring at the piece of dried
up cheese in the fridge...

YABBIE
COTTAGE
RESTAURANT
—
AUTHENTIC
DROUGHT
CUISINE

I DECLARE THIS TIN
OF BAKED BEANS WELL
AND TRULY OPEN...

CLOUD
ON A
STICK
10¢

BAN
LIVE
ANIMAL
EXPORT

May I have the
pleasure of the next
sadly outdated
courting ritual...

NO DEPOSIT

MUNGO'S GOLDEN PHEASANT

Here **I** am...
UNEMPLOYED...
UNIMPORTANT...

And there **you** ARE...
WEALTHY....
POWERFUL...

YOU OWN
PROPERTY... GOLD...
ART.... WINE AND
HUMAN SOULS IN
MASSIVE, SICKENING,
CRIMINAL QUANTITIES...!

HOW DO YOU
SLEEP AT
NIGHT..?

I sleep at night
between silk sheets on
a heated, king size
auto-massage water bed with
piped music in a very
quiet street...

... with a companion
whose beauty would
make you weep with
desire....

Leuny

Now I lay me down to sleep
I pray thee Lord my soul to sweep
Yes sweep it with your mighty broom
Until it's like a tidy room
All neat and clean with doors shut tight
And curtains drawn against the light
The neatest, darkest piece of gloom
My soul, my locked and empty room.

BAN
MESSAGE
T-SHIRTS

CULPRIT

Once upon a time white people had sacred sites and a dreamtime.

All this was eventually subdivided.

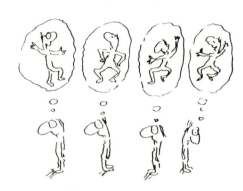

Such a subdivision is now called PRIVACY.

This is where the human spirit lives in such solitary confinement.....

.... that it becomes INDIVIDUALITY....

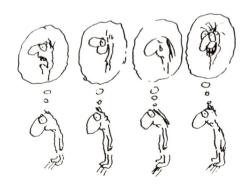

... and individuality becomes a secret which is carried to the grave.

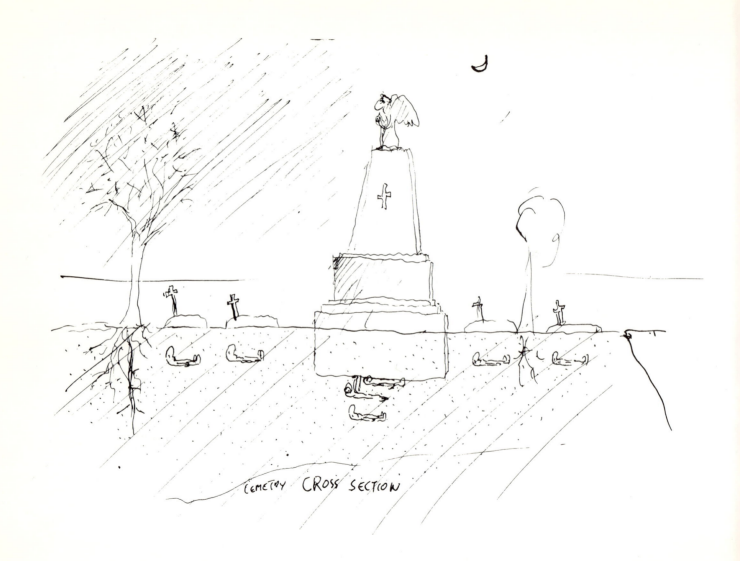

CEMETRY CROSS SECTION

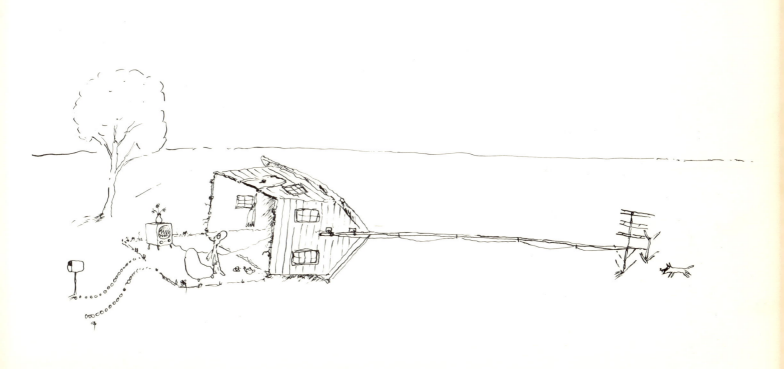

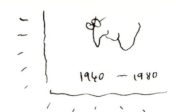

1940 — 1980

WHO'S GOING
TO WRITE THE
POETRY OF OUR
OLD AGE...?

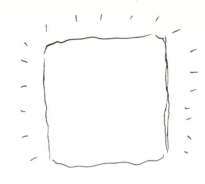

IMAGINE THERE'S
NO JOHN LENNON...
THAT MAN WROTE THE
POETRY OF OUR YOUTH..

I IMAGINE
THERE'S NOTHING
VERY POETIC ABOUT
SENILE DECAY

This canary you sold me... He won't sing... HE WEEPS...!

He sits on his perch all day... WEEPING and SOBBING...!

That's because he's a modern urban canary... he's educated... aware... sensitive ... liberated... artistic... and he also likes the sound of breaking glass...

That's how they sing... these days.. They sing the BLUES

WONDERFUL EARLY WARNING Devices,... Canaries.

Leunig

"Please trust us . . . we're not trying to convert you . . . we only want to help you."

THE HAPPY PRINCE

ONCE UPON A TIME IN THE TOWN SQUARE THERE WAS A MEANINGFUL STATUE CALLED THE HAPPY PRINCE.

AN ARTIST WHO WAS FLYING AWAY FROM THE ONSET OF CONFUSION ALIGHTED TO REST ON THE SHOULDER OF THE HAPPY PRINCE.

THE STATUE SPOKE TO THE ARTIST. "THERE ARE MANY BEWILDERED PEOPLE IN THIS TOWN... STRIP AWAY MY MEANING AND TAKE IT TO THEM."

SO THE ARTIST BEGAN TO STRIP AWAY THE MEANINGFUL FEATURES AND TAKE THEM TO THE PEOPLE

"YOU MUST HURRY" SAID THE HAPPY PRINCE "OR YOU WILL BE CAUGHT UP IN THE GROWING CONFUSION"

BUT THE ARTIST CONTINUED FEARLESSLY UNTIL ALL THAT WAS LEFT OF THE HAPPY PRINCE WAS THE NAKED HEART.

THE TOWN'S PEOPLE DID NOT UNDERSTAND HEARTS VERY WELL AND WERE ANGERED AND EMBARRASSED BY THE SIGHT OF IT....

AND THE ARTIST FELL DOWN TOO EXHAUSTED TO CONTINUE HIS FLIGHT TO SIMPLICITY.

THE TOWN COUNCIL ORDERED THE HEART TO BE REMOVED AND REPLACED WITH SOMETHING WHICH COULD BE UNDERSTOOD.

BUT NOTHING COULD HALT THE ONSET OF CONFUSION AND MEANINGLESSNESS...

NOTHING... EXCEPT A SENSE OF MYSTERY WHICH NURTURED THE ARTIST AND THE EXILED HEART OF THE HAPPY PRINCE.

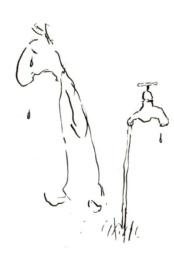

Down I lay in a boat on the bay
And I dreamed about friends of the past
And while I was sleeping
The dream upward creeping
Had fastened itself to the mast

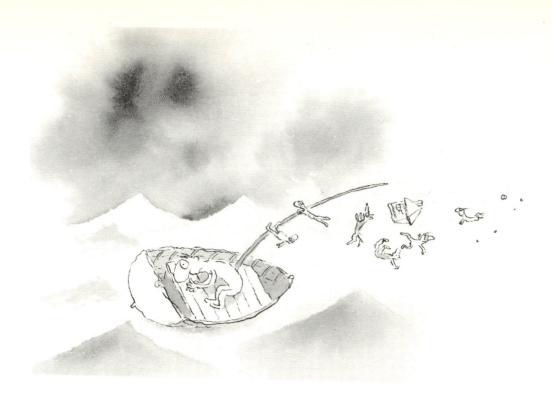

So blow all ye gales and fill up my sails
And carry me far, far away.
'Til my billowing dreams
All burst at the seams
As I lie in a boat on the bay.

ON A SUMMER'S EVENING MR. CURLY ARRIVES AT THE
HIATUS HOTEL FOR A NIGHT OF AMUSEMENT AND ROMANCE.
THE DUCKHERD WAVES... THE PALMS RUSTLE IN THE
BALMY BREEZE... A MANDOLIN PLAYS... GLASSES TINKLE..
LAUGHTER... KISSES... ON AND ON... OVER AND OVER... LIFE IS JOYOUS.   Leunig